.

Bumwigs and Earbeetles
and other Unspeakable Delights

Bumwigs and Earbeetles
and other Unspeakable Delights

poems by
Ann Ziety

The Bodley Head

London

Bumwigs and Earbeetles and other Unspeakable Delights

1 3 5 7 9 10 8 6 4 2

Copyright © text Wendy Metcalf 1995
Copyright © illustrations Lesley Bisseker 1995

Wendy Metcalf and Lesley Bisseker have asserted their rights under the Copyright, Designs and Patents Act, 1988 to be identified as the author and illustrator of this work

First published in the United Kingdom 1995
by The Bodley Head Children's Books
Random House, 20 Vauxhall Bridge Road, London SW1V 2SA

Random House Australia (Pty) Limited
20 Alfred Street, Milsons Point, Sydney,
New South Wales 2061, Australia

Random House New Zealand Limited
18 Poland Road, Glenfield,
Auckland 10, New Zealand

Random House South Africa (Pty) Limited
PO Box 337, Bergvlei 2012, South Africa

Random House UK Limited Reg. No. 954009

A CIP record for this book is available from the British Library

ISBN 0 370 31975 3

Printed and bound in Great Britain by
Mackays of Chatham PLC, Chatham, Kent

CONTENTS

Anatomy of a Poet	1
Grandad's Compost Heap	3
Neighbours	6
Bath-Time	8
Micky Martin's Nose	10
Buy One – Get One Free	12
My Dog Never Had Fleas	15
Marcus Henry Postlethwaite-Carruthers-de-la-Snobbe	18
Beryl The Budgie	20
Pullover	22
Washing Up	24
Symbiosis	26
Sellotape	29
Success	31
Catfood	32
Av a Butty	34
Semolina	36
Uncle Simon's Stomach	38
My Granny	42
Bubble Poem	44
Problems With Spaghetti	46
The Dustbin Liner	48
Fatty the Cat	50
Laundry Poem	54
Fast Food	56
Celebration	57
At The Bottom	58
Two's Company	61
Nobody	62
Statistics	63
Knit-One Pearl-One	64
Computer	66
Jigsaw	68
Last Day in Broadstairs	69
A Loss	70
National Poetry Day	72

ANATOMY OF A POET

her footle is connected
to her frumpy-rumple-doo
which conspirigates itself around
her antiperspypoo
her post-lymphatic gangeroids
located in each ear
avoid her situponicles
located in the rear
her polyglotic femuroidal
sophoglatic phlange
hangs very loosely in between
and guards against the mange
her angeroidal metacarpis
just above the chest
contracts to hyperventilate
and aeriates her vest
constricted by contabulations
round about the heart
are brillopaddic bumbly-tracts
which meet then fall apart
her streptopickle-plonking button
just below the ribs
recedes in stormy weather
or when she's telling fibs
her cybernetic clacker-wibble
wobbles when she walks
her tackytetro-telemachus
giggles when she talks
her secondary pontefract
pulsating near the spleen
emits a pulmonary spray
and turns a putrid green
her vacillating vladivostok
often lying dormant
is known to burst its bladderbog
and cause a sudden torment
her catalytic shifter
which is often out of use

installs itself quite neatly
in her Ashby-De-La-Zouche
her megalythic marlybone
is just like yours or mine
and it swivels in a socket
at the bottom of her spine
at dinner-time her heebiegeebie
gastronominater
consolidates her consommé
and purifies it later
but
her poetetic persiflage
is what she uses best
that's the bit that writes the poems
and it never takes a rest

GRANDAD'S COMPOST HEAP

us kids loved to play out
on Grandad's compost heap

it was a mountain of methane
in the corner of the yard
and we'd be out there till dusk
chuckin' rotten egg shells
and old tea bags at one another
sliding around on slopes of slippery peelings
and God knows what

we never used to go out stealing
and getting into trouble
we were too happy playin' int' muck
getting marmite and jam stains on us clogs
and chocolate and trifle stains on us trousers

come Christmas time
we never had presents
we didn't need presents
all we wanted was to go ont' compost
and gerra bit smelly
slithering amongst the slivers of carrot scrapings
rancid yoghurt blobs, past-it pasties
historic chutney and putrefactive fish heads

you had real games in them days

we used to play catch wi' old faggots
and football wi' disintegrating cabbage
our dolls were made from chicken carcasses
with turnip heads and chips for arms and legs
our books were soggy biscuit wrappings
and newsprint fromt' bottom o' the budgie's cage
we'd have ash and semolina fights
and we'd clonk each other overt' head
wi' old mutton bones and legs o' lamb

we'd take yards and yards of cold spaghetti
and knit it into skipping ropes
to squelchily jump to our favourite rhymes:
   'Is it a pie, or is it a pastie,
   I just trod in something nasty
   Out Goes You!'

and for skates you'd rub beef drippin'
ont' bottom of your clogs
and slide about like Torville and Dean

ont' birthday
as a special treat
you used to turn the compost
with Grandad's huge shovel
over and over
steamier and steamier
till you got to the very bottom
where cadaverous ancient life forms
wiggled their antennae at you
in the dark primeval soup
and everybody came out and had a go
bringing along bags of horse manure
leftover catfood
and spoils from the sink-tidy
there'd be Aunty Bea with her old rice puddin'
and Grandma Ziety with a few dead sparrers
and we'd all join hands
and dance roundt' compost
and have a real singsong
till it were time for bed

we didn't have much
but we were happy
you made your own fun in them days

telly's killed all that

NEIGHBOURS

when the sun shines bright
and the grass is tall
and there are full fat berries in the hedgerows
and the skylark sings its one true note
and every garden is hushed and still
and the loving arms of a willow tree
hang by the water's edge
and the dragonflies dip their rainbow bodies
and dart with silent stealth

when the blessing falls
and the buttercups glow
and the clouds sit happy and smugly still
and your heart sings like an evening swallow
as peace descends like a gentle kiss

there is always someone
next door
with a buzz saw
or a power drill
or a lawn mower
going

BZZZZZZZZRRRRRRRZZZZZZGHHHH!!!!!!!!!

BATH-TIME

bath-time wasn't easy
with seventeen of us
and the dog
plus we'd throw the goldfish in
to give him a good swim

we were deprived of bubbles
suds and bath-oils
no avocado and chocolate mousse shampoo for us
no namby-pamby eau de toilette
Mam used to throw in a bit of bleach
to make us come out rosy

rubber ducks were considered a luxury
so we floated the frozen chicken
for tomorrow's Sunday dinner
and torpedoed it with loofers

getting dry was difficult with only one tea-towel
no fire
and a hole in the roof

we'd sit round a candle and tell stories
while the hole let in the starlight
and the soot from nextdoor's chimney
that covered us from head to foot
in black, burnt dirt

'Just look at the state of you,' Mam would say,
'You need a good bath!'

MICKY MARTIN'S NOSE

Bicky Bartin had a doze
bunged
blocked
barricaded
with adenoidal problebs

he was uncobbenly biserable
for subwob of his age

his putty-like protruberance
his rhinocerotic conklette
gleamed red and purple
sniffed without hope
through dark and dessicated nostril-holes

asybbetric nozzle-blower
constipated spiracle
this floundering sniffysnout of flattened flesh
coated itself often
in ice creab, candyfloss
and chocolate bilkshake,
hung with dewdrops on a winter's day
and sang a sinusitis song of snuffles
when Bicky Bartin went to bed and slept

bubulous and treblified
this adenoidal aubergine
this unhobogenous hooter
though biserable when breathing air
could play ibaginative tunes
if Bicky held one nostril down
and blew with bronchial vigour:
high-pitched whistling wheezicles
trilled and thrupped and thrippled out
in nasalotic cadences
it was The Sound of Mucus!

thrippy-thrup went Bicky's doze
in tempos wild and strong
and everyone would sing along
to Bicky Bartin's sybphony
to Bicky's snitch of perfect pitch
to Bicky's special song

thrippy-thrup
and thruppy-thrip
went the strange rhapsnotic sound
like a hoover sucking soup
thrippy-thrup
and thruppy-throop
the dogs all came from miles around
the cats would shriek and flex their claws
and everybody jumped and jived
and all the world gave loud applause
to Bicky's song of sweet repose
to Bicky's scaly, ailing, failing
Vic-inhaling doze

BUY ONE – GET ONE FREE

Salesman came knocking on my door one day
He crept up the drive like a winter fog
I opened the entrance to my secret home
And there he stood with his catalogue
Of everything that ever was
For anyone who cares to see:
   'BUY ONE – GET ONE FREE'

Salesman scratches and shuffling his feet
Gives a yawn like an open toilet seat
Fumbles for leaflets on casserole dishes
Asks if I'm into tropical fishes
Brings out a picture of a copper-bottomed frying
   pan
Tries to do a bad impersonation of an honest man
Smiles like a housewife on a spending spree
Has to remind me:
   'BUY ONE – GET ONE FREE'

T-shirts reading 'I am Barmy'
Special offer biriani
Band aids slimming aids first aid orangeade
Jugs mugs plugs rugs, shirts that never fade
Elasticated dog leads, underwear to last yer
Packets of spaghetti and squiggly bits of pasta
Ointment for lumps bumps and balding cats
Polish for woodwork and souvenir cricket bats
Red wigs dried figs cheap cigs CB rigs
Everything's under guarantee:
   'BUY ONE – GET ONE FREE'

Wedding dresses for the bride
Pet gnus with pesticide
Japanese kamikaze helmets
Cotton towels and curtain pelmets
Do-It-Yourself appendectomy kits
This and that and bobs and bits
Fur-lined knickers by Christian Dior:
   'BUY THREE – GET THREE MORE'

So now my home is full of books
And clothes and shoes and curtain hooks
And several pairs of stripy long johns
And bed-caps sporting dangly pom-poms
Clocks and socks and safety locks
China cups and Chinese woks
Nicks and nacks and nails and nobs
Pieces of string and thingiemabobs
Oojemaflips and whatsernames
Party hats and picture frames
Potted plants and padded bras
Miscellaneous etceteras

The house is full – so that is that
I'm sleeping in the laundromat
There's never enough room you see
To BUY ONE – GET ONE FREE

MY DOG NEVER HAD FLEAS

my dog never had fleas

he had bumwigs and earbeetles
and sinus larvae
and one or two exaggerated boils
and bits of ticks that stuck to his ears
and sticky mites
and bites from fights
and stashes and stashes of nasty rashes
but he never had fleas
not one

when I took him for walks
he snuffled through rubbish tips
and caught things on his way home
when they saw him, viruses used to shout:
'Yippeeee! Here's dinner and Black Death
all rolled into one!'
but he ambled on, carelessly snuffling the
 bogmoss
and disappearing under piles of leaves
to emerge with more bald patches
exposed in the dying sun
he had an awful skin disease
but he never had fleas
not one

when he grew old
and suffered
from a gnostric inflammatory gumboil
that he caught off a fieldmouse
in the Autumn of 1973
I took him to the vets
and that was when we found the zicks
and the thundercrabs
and the vascular tiddlesuckers
and the molar widges and big red wip-waps
and purply bungflies with hairy mandibles

chomping and nibbling and slurping and burping
and clusters of slug and shoals of grumblesnits
and mangy, gangreeny nostril grubs
like the ones I once found in my Chelsea bun
   yurrrrrghhhhh!!!
we found all of these beyond normal treatment
we even found a smattering of Dutch Elm disease
but we never found fleas
not one

my dear old spitty dog
dragged on till he was twenty-three
with a wobbly tum
but at least regurgitation was easy
and lots and lots of mouldy warts
which he got through eating a dead weasel
in the Cotswolds
on one of our strenuous winter walks

and when the last winds blew around his tufts
he closed the one eye he had left
and lay down on a dungpile
to dream forever

he'd had a good life of variety and fun
he'd had weals and blotches
and globular notches
and piles and styes
and wheezes and sneezes
and snuffles and truffles
and squirtings and scurvy bits
but he never had fleas
not one

MARCUS HENRY POSTLETHWAITE-CARRUTHERS-DE-LA-SNOBBE

Ay've got an Applemac
Ay've got a rich dad
Ay've got a long name
Ay've got a long laugh
Ay go Haw Haw
Haw Haw Haw Haw
Haw Haw Haw
when ay see somebody poor

We've got a library
We've got a big car
We've got a big house
In Bromley not in Brixton
We eat caviar
Camembert and canapés
We shop at Harrods
For a better class of person
We go Haw Haw
Haw Haw Haw Haw
Haw Haw Haw
When we see somebody poor

Ay've got a snub nose
Ay've got a smart suit
Ay look like a newt
That's swallowed its tonsils
Ay've got a keen brain
Ay've got a clean bum
Ay pull may socks up
And sharpen may pencils

Ay'm Mummy's favourite
Ay'm going to Cambridge
Ay'm going to learn about
The poor being smelly
Ay want to go far
Ay'm going to work hard
Then when ay'm famous
You'll see me on the telly
Ay'll go Haw Haw
Haw Haw Haw Haw
Haw Haw Haw
When ay talk about the poor

Ay've never longed for
A book or a bicycle
Ay've never yearned for
May dad to find a job
No, ay've never wanted
Or wished for a thing
Cos ay'm
MARCUS
HENRY
POSTLETHWAITE-CARRUTHERS
DE-LA-SNOBBE

Ay've got a future
Ay've got a big plan
Ay'll be Prime Minister
In twenty-twenty-four
And ay'll go Haw Haw
Haw Haw Haw Haw
Haw Haw Haw Haw
HAW HAW HAW

BERYL THE BUDGIE

Our budgie suffered from depression
huddled
hunched-over
cramped into the corner of the cage
she never talked or whistled
just stared blankly
at a world of plastic toys

being called Beryl didn't help much, either

'Females don't talk,' the vet said
'They just lay eggs'

so we gave her a nest to sit on
and plenty of birdseed
but it didn't help
she still had a face as long
as a wet weekend in Wolverhampton

every day we'd poke her about a bit
and jolly her along with little songs
and nursery rhymes
and call her 'Pretty Beryl'
'Clever Beryl'
'Beryl sing for Mummy, sing for Daddy, do'
'Beryl inky binky boo!'

one day, after much encouragement
Beryl opened her little beak and spoke:
'WHY DON'T YOU ALL NAFF OFF
AND LEAVE ME ALONE!' she said

it was a great moment for all of us

PULLOVER

long ago
when the earth was full of darkness
and primeval creatures heaved and pushed
their bulky bodies through the seething swamps
and mud bubbled and spewed its sulphurous
   soup
up through the boiling caverns of volcanic rock
my pullover evolved
slowly
shapeless and heaving
a dreary mass of convoluted cable-stitch
a crawling off-the-shoulder teabag
terrible and vile

sponge for rampant spillages
and diabolic dinner-droppings
my pullover clawed its ceaseless way through
   forests
squelched through muddy streams
and scraggily attempted mountain passes
writhed in grimy greasy gravy lakes
and plunged itself in scarlet pools of ketchup
with deep howlings of despair

spotted
splodged on
squished with orange squash and coffee-slops
it stopped at nothing
till it found me
(via Aunty Patsy as a Christmas present)
and became
the THING I wear

formed by the couplings of organic fungus clusters
this woolly wadge of Fair Isle formlessness
had dragged its ragged torso through the
   centuries

scrabbled the rough rocks and spikey stalagtites
frayed and frazzled by frantic gnat-nibblings
unravelled by time and tattered by hurricanes
it came to me from out of the darkness
rested its arms (too short) upon my arms
and put its waist (too long) around my waist
and smothered my small and slender frame
in unfashionable bunny motifs
green puce red purple
with gratuitous blobby bits that wobbled when I
  walked
I looked like a psychedelic warty marquee

and everybody said how much it suited me

WASHING UP

Wendy's washing up again
Wendy's washing up again

John goes out and drives a tank
Burt is busy at the bank
Tim goes out and drives a train
And Wendy's washing up again

Frank is flying to the moon
Hank will get promotion soon
Freddie likes to fly a plane
And Wendy's washing up again

Danny drives a racing car
Gordon plays a mean guitar
Cyril cycles down the lane
And Wendy's washing up again

Oh dear, where has Wendy gone?
Has she left with Burt and John?
Is she flying through the air
Could it be she's having fun?

Tim and John and Burt and Frank
Seem quite worried – so is Hank
They stare at every plate and cup
Now who will do the washing up?
Now who will do the washing up?

SYMBIOSIS

the beard beetle lives
on beer-froth and beef broth
and snortings of soup-spillage
snaffles of wafer
it hides in the forest
of infinite sproutings
it lies in the jungle
of tortuous tangles
meandering idly
through bristles and prickles
it gathers the toast-crumbs
and cruddies of biscuit
it harvests the dustmites
and slavers the Brylcream
it nibbles on split ends
and crochets the fibres
and whoozily snoozes
on soft dunes of dandruff
and tickles its fancy
with flyaway hairwisps

curling in curlicue crumples of fuzz
the beard beetle potters
through tatters of tangle
through snitters of matting
through clusters of lug
it forays through follicles
popping up nostril-holes
hopping on chin-weevils
nestling in squiggliness
whistling its happiness
proud of its messiness
gobbling up gone-astray
toothpaste and peas
it macramés the loose hair
with angular mandibles
weaving small duvets
with notable zeal

creating constructions
and knotty concoctions
of artistic merit
and instant appeal

the beard beetle nestles
on my Uncle Colin
who lives off Aunt Patsy
who lives off her pension

which comes from the Social
which asks lots of questions
which chivies and bullies
and potters through personal
feelings and histories
wearily worrying
busily badgering
nosing and nosing
for names and addresses
it chunders the numbers
with rascally relish
it *col*lates and *cal*culates
costs and entitlements
slurping the data
digesting the facts
it feeds Aunty Patsy
who feeds Uncle Colin
who dribbles his cocoa
and drools tapioca
which trickles down slowly
through layers of bristle
in seepings and creepings
to nurture the beetle
who silent and secret
has beaten the system
too small to be noticed
too strange to be real
it suctions the handouts
of plentiful ploppings
it siphons the succulent
sippings and suckings
it never feels guilty
for slobbily slobbing
gives thanks for its lot
and enjoys every meal

SELLOTAPE

I can stick things down
I can wrap things up
Everybody knows it's great
I can make things come together
With my roll of Sellotape

If you're feeling down
Or a bit fed up
And you've too much on your plate
I can help you keep your pecker up
With my Sellotape

I can mend a friend who's on the dole
I can mend a broken heart
I can stick your bits all back together
When they fall apart

Oh, I'm ready for a nuclear war
Or a nuclear mistake
And I won't need a bunker underground
Cos I've got my Sellotape

If you've got a piece that's hangin' funny –
Maybe a broken leg
Don't bother seeing the doctor, Honey
I'll patch you up instead

Oh, the Leaning Tower of Pisa
Could be really rather straight
If they'd only let me have a go
With my Sellotape

If you've got a piece that's sort of dangly –
Maybe its day is done
Don't bother seeing the doctor, Stanley
I'll Sellotape it on!

I can stick things down
I can wrap things up
Everybody knows it's great
I can make things come together
With my roll of Sellotape

SUCCESS

Jenny had a bank account
Jilly had a kite
Jenny worked and worked and worked
Jilly rode her bike
Jenny had a smart suit
Jilly had split ends
Jenny had a job in Sales
Jilly laughed with all her friends
Jenny had a future
Jilly's debts were growing
Jenny made investments
Jilly wrote a poem
Jenny grew to be quite rich
Jilly grew quite poor
Then Jenny had a heart attack
When she was forty-four

CATFOOD

Chewsy Chops and Mewsy Meat
Chombly Chunks and Chumbly Beef
Licky Lamb and Catty Clumps
Iddums-Diddums-Liver-Lumps
Kittenbits and Kattobites
Nummy Yum and Nicey Nice
Whisker Wumps and Kidney Wipes
Mousey Mince and Mincey Mites
Snacky Snicks and Beefy Bites
Tiddles Treats and Tabby Snacks
Rabbit Scrag and Scraggy Snaps
Piggy Squigs and Pukey Pops
Pancreatic Gristle-Chops
Camel Humps and Bacon Blobs
Pussy Piles and Gastro Gobs
Rubber Parts and Blubber Bliss

Would you feed your cat on this?

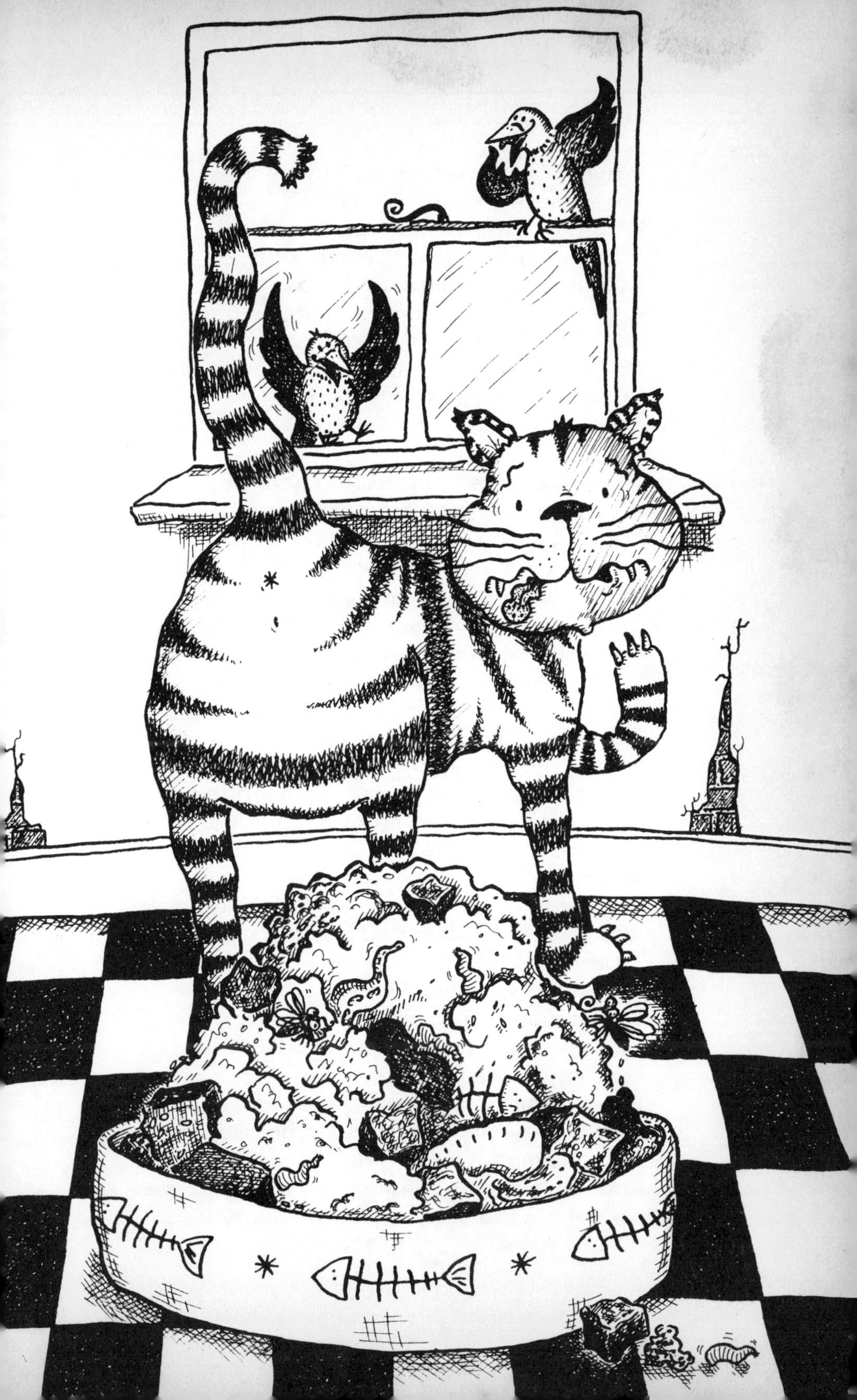

AV A BUTTY

When Gilliam was five and I was three
We went to visit my Aunty Bea
Who gave us cakes and cups of tea
And sat us down on her big settee
But I got too excited at half-past four
And made a mess on the bathroom floor
I cried and cried and cried and cried
And felt so embarrassed I could have died
But Aunty Bea just said to me
   'Ne'er mind luv, av a butty'

When we were older, Gillian and me
We courted lots of boys and acne
And got stood up and got let down
And stood in bars and spoke to bores
Who made us yawn and yawn and yawn
And Gillian wished she had never been born
So we crawled our way to Aunty Bea
   Who said 'Ne'er mind, av a butty'

Then we graduated, fully educated
Newly emancipated, quite elated
Eager to rummage through the world outside
And I tried and tried and tried and tried
To make the grade and wear a skirt
And bake a cake and marry Burt
But the chains creaked and the locks rattled
And the doors slammed and the neighbours
   prattled
So I stayed a while with Aunty Bea
   Who said 'Ne'er mind, av a butty'

My friend Gillian's got it made
She's gone to live in Adelaide
With her gynaecologist husband, George
And she isn't even slightly bored
And she says she sometimes thinks of me
And of course she misses my Aunty Bea

Who died a while back
Sudden-like
In the middle of the night

I wonder why

Whenever I eat a ham butty now
I cry and cry and cry and cry
Cos Aunty Bea was like a mother
Then I shrug my shoulders
And av another

SEMOLINA

Edwina lived on Semolina
Semolina's what she liked
Semolina in the bath
Semolina on a bike
Semolina by a stream
Semolina in her bed
At night Edwina used to dream
Of Semolina in Hampstead

Semolina by the telly
Semolina in the rain
Semolina mixed with jam
Or Semolina plain
Semolina at the office
Semolina at the bank
Semolina in a car
Semolina on a tank
Semolina on a train
Semolina from the can
At night Edwina used to dream
Of her Semolina man

One day she met him eating
Semolina on the Scilly Isles
They had two lovely children
With Semolina smiles
They bought a Semolina house
In Semolina Surrey Docks
She cooked him Semolina
Darned his Semolina socks
They met some Semolina friends
And had a spiffing time
Giving Semolina parties
With Semolina wine

Edwina lived on Semolina
Semolina's what she liked
Semolina in the bath
Semolina on a bike
Semolina by a stream
Semolina in her bed
At night Edwina used to dream
Of Semolina in Hampstead
Until one day Edwina said
I fancy strawberries and cream
Semolina I'm ignoring
Cos Semolina's boring

UNCLE SIMON'S STOMACH

Uncle Simon's stomach
was big as a planet
the biggest stomach
in Stoke Newington

when I was three
he'd let me lie on it
and pressing my ear close to his inner workings
I marvelled at a plughole symphony of squeakings
I could hear the sure, slow destruction
of pea and ham soup
pork pie and chips
a cup of tea and two scones
and last night's boiled bacon butties with English
 mustard

the music of his alimentary waterways
the chirrup of his warped internal plumbing
sent me into a state of dreamy rapture
my ear moved from stomach down to abdomen
following the flow of pancreatic juices
the cascade of duodenal dowsings
and thrilled to the jiggly-plop and rumble
of his great gymnastic colon
wheezing like a blocked drain in a disused mansion

once
at Auntie Sharon's Silver Wedding party
after sixteen prawn vol-au-vents
and three pints of Guinness
such grandiose pickling sounds rent my ear
relentless acid-squirtings, spleenal seepings
followed by thunder and lightning
squally showers, wind and hail

my own particular favourite
was chicken biriani with lime pickle:

cannon-fire
the sound of a rushing sea
the thundering hooves of a million stampeding
   buffalo
and a beagle-hound howling on a stormy night

here was no ordinary boring belly
no delicate or sensitive tum-tum this
but a madly churning indiscriminate cement mixer
a full-bodied rugby-scrum of squealing enzymes

it was when we could hear the 1812 overture
played loud and backwards
that we got the doctor in
and I heard the gluey medicine go down
and what I thought was the unstoppable force of
   life
was turned off like a tap
and all was still and gloom-quiet

it was never the same after that
no more large colon juggling with liquefied
   sandwiches
no more relentless breakdown of brittle Bourbon
   biscuits
just the quiet drip drip of a tamed digestion:
liver, spleen, kidneys, gall bladder
all working together in tranquil harmony
like a silent tennis match with no spectators
a sleeping umpire and no ball

but there were relapses

and the chance to hear a trumpet voluntary
played in D Major on the duodenum
accompanied by a strained appendix, a whistling
   spleen
and backed by a heavenly chorus of soupy
   hallelujahs
as Uncle Simon spoke his final words:

'What's for puddin'?'

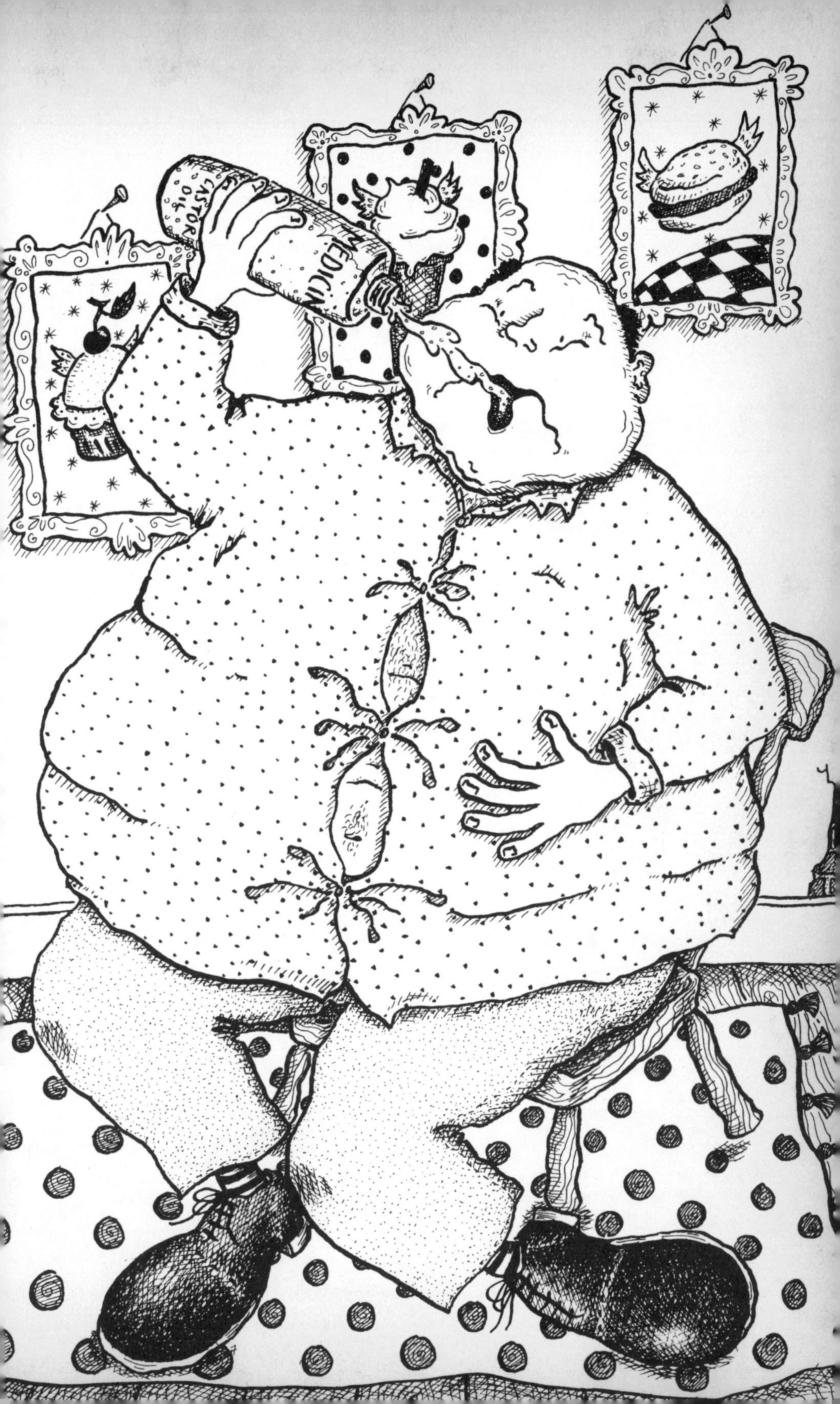
CASTOR OIL
MEDICIN

MY GRANNY

Some grannies are knitters, some grannies make hats
Some grannies smoke kippers, some grannies keep cats
Some grannies have gardens and some live in flats
Buy my Granny's a lumberjack
How about that!

She never stays in on a Saturday night
She goes to the woods on her big mountain bike
And she chops down the trees with a thud and a thwack
Cos my Granny's a lumberjack
How about that!

The neighbours all think that my Granny is bonkers
She goes to the forest to rummage for conkers
Then she gets out her buzz saw and suddenly CRACK!
Cos my Granny's a lumberjack
How about that!

She loves to go out when the weather is fine
And the sweet air is rich with the fresh smell of pine
As she clears up the forest with Chuck and Big Matt
Cos my Granny's a lumberjack
How about that!

Don't tell her she's old and don't tell her she's mad
Don't say all this dumb lumberjacking's a fad
Or she'll get out her buzz saw and suddenly SPLAT!
Cos my Granny's a lumberjack
How about that!

BUBBLE POEM

When my head is full of troubles
And my heart is full of care
I blow bubbles
Lovely bubbles
Floating floating in the air

When the world is harsh and angry
And nobody seems to care
I blow bubbles
Rainbow bubbles
Floating floating everywhere

Bubbles always make us happy
When we find it hard to cope
For inside each perfect circle
Lies a little ray of hope

When the night is dark and lonely
And the shadows make you cry
Just blow bubbles
Rainbow bubbles
Floating floating in the sky

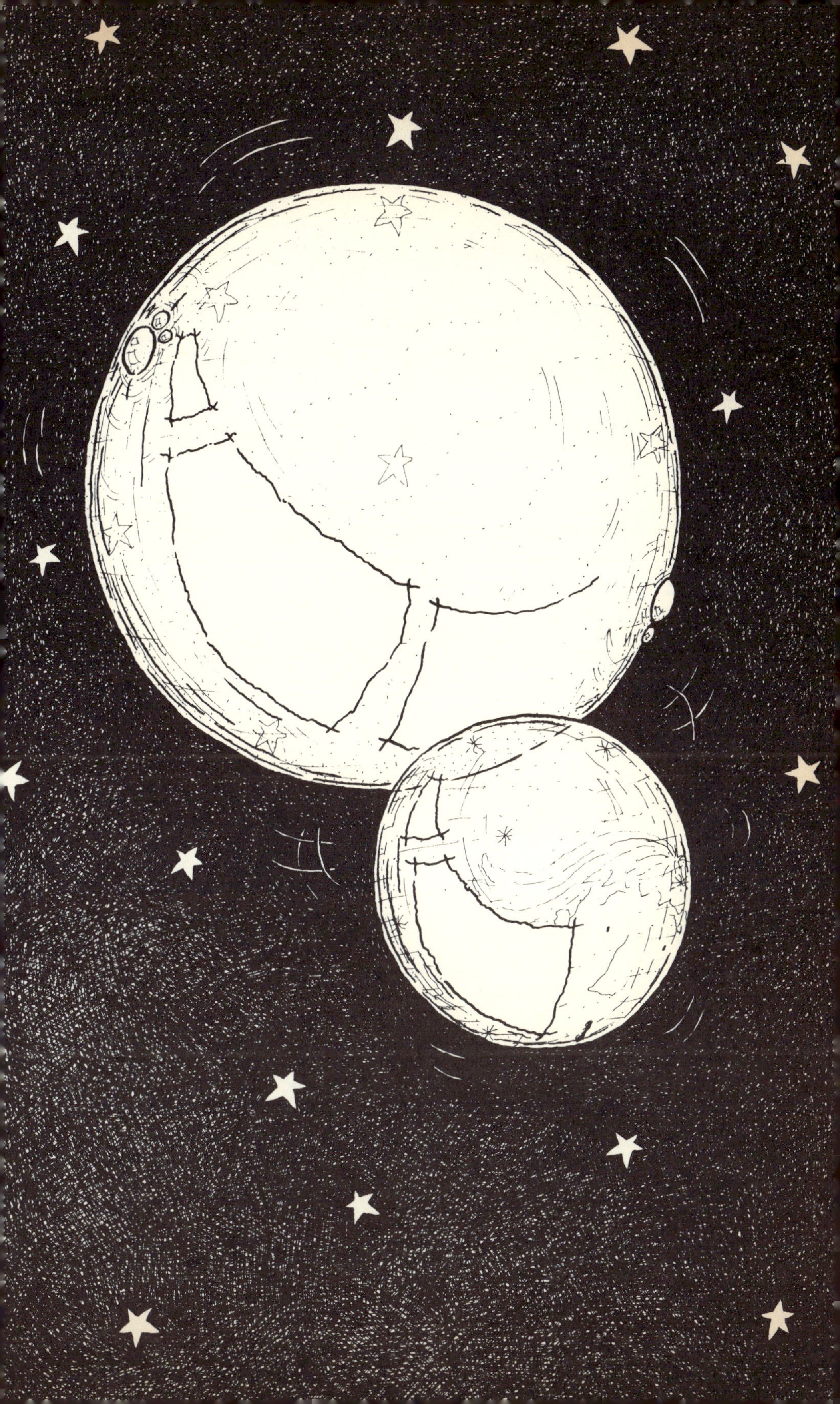

PROBLEMS WITH SPAGHETTI

Grandma Ziety
couldn't eat spaghetti
on account of her dentures

so she knitted with it
and crocheted
spaghetti socks
jumpers
coverlets
and a spaghetti singlet for the dog

when hoops came out in cans
she spat at supermarket checkout girl, Sandra
and said
'How'm I supposed ter make a Balaclava outter
   this?'

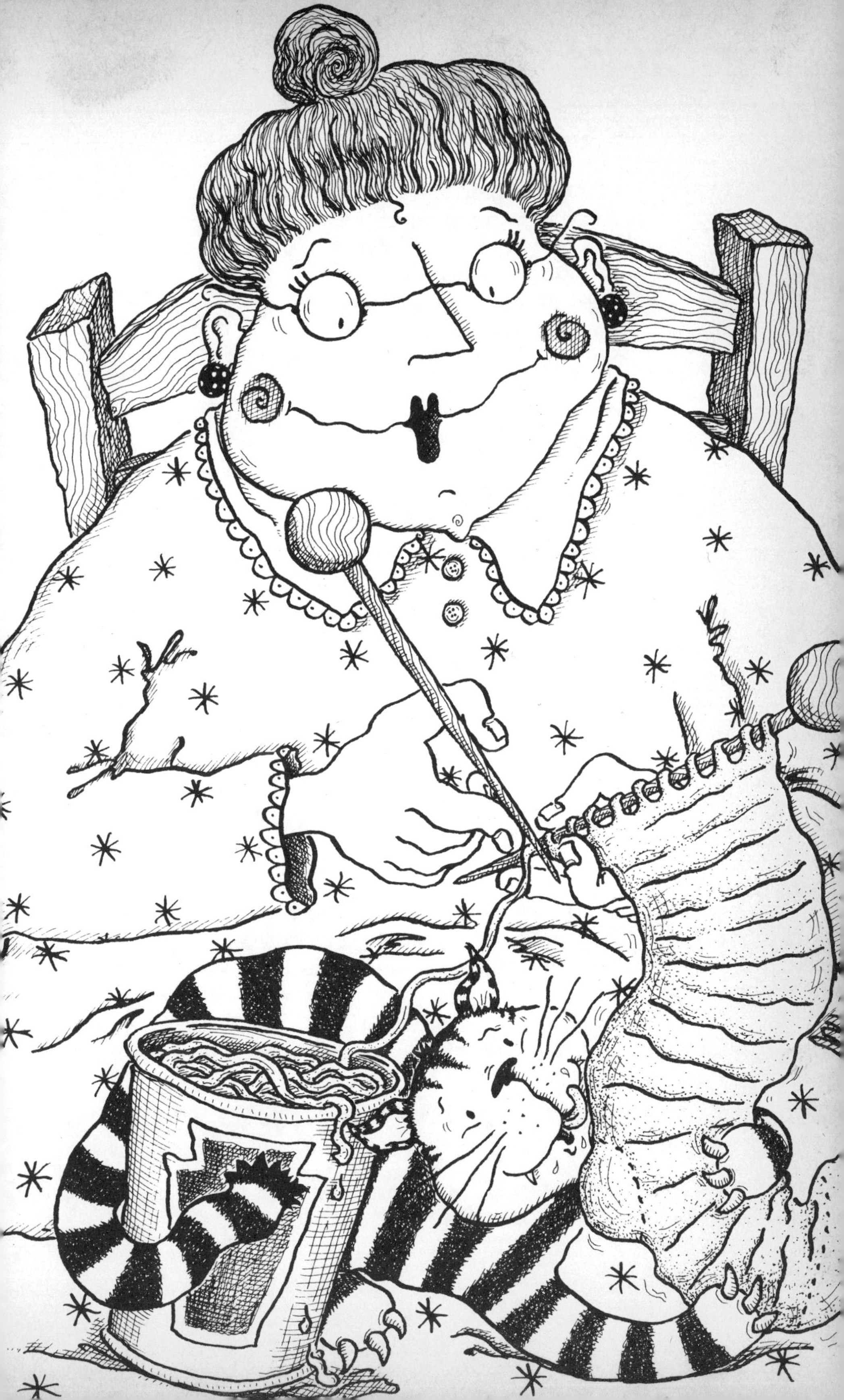

THE DUSTBIN LINER

I've got a glorious dustbin liner
Filled with unspeakable things:
I've got an old pet parrot
A decomposing carrot
A lot of squashy squishy
Some coagulated icky
And the bones of twenty-five chicken wings

I've got some cold Heinz spaghetti
A hairy semolina
A past-it pastie and a cluster of goo
A bottle of Ribena
The droppings of a ferret
My Granny's old hanky
And some stale home brew

I've got a sludgified tomato
A sloppy slippy omelette
A smelly rubber tyre
And a bit of mushy splosh
The dust from the hoover
Some rancid wart remover
And a long string vest
That has never been washed

Here is my glorious dustbin liner
Filled with unspeakable things:
Oh yes, it also contains a very lively,
very hungry, very enormous
SQUID
If you will put your head in it
I will give you fifty quid

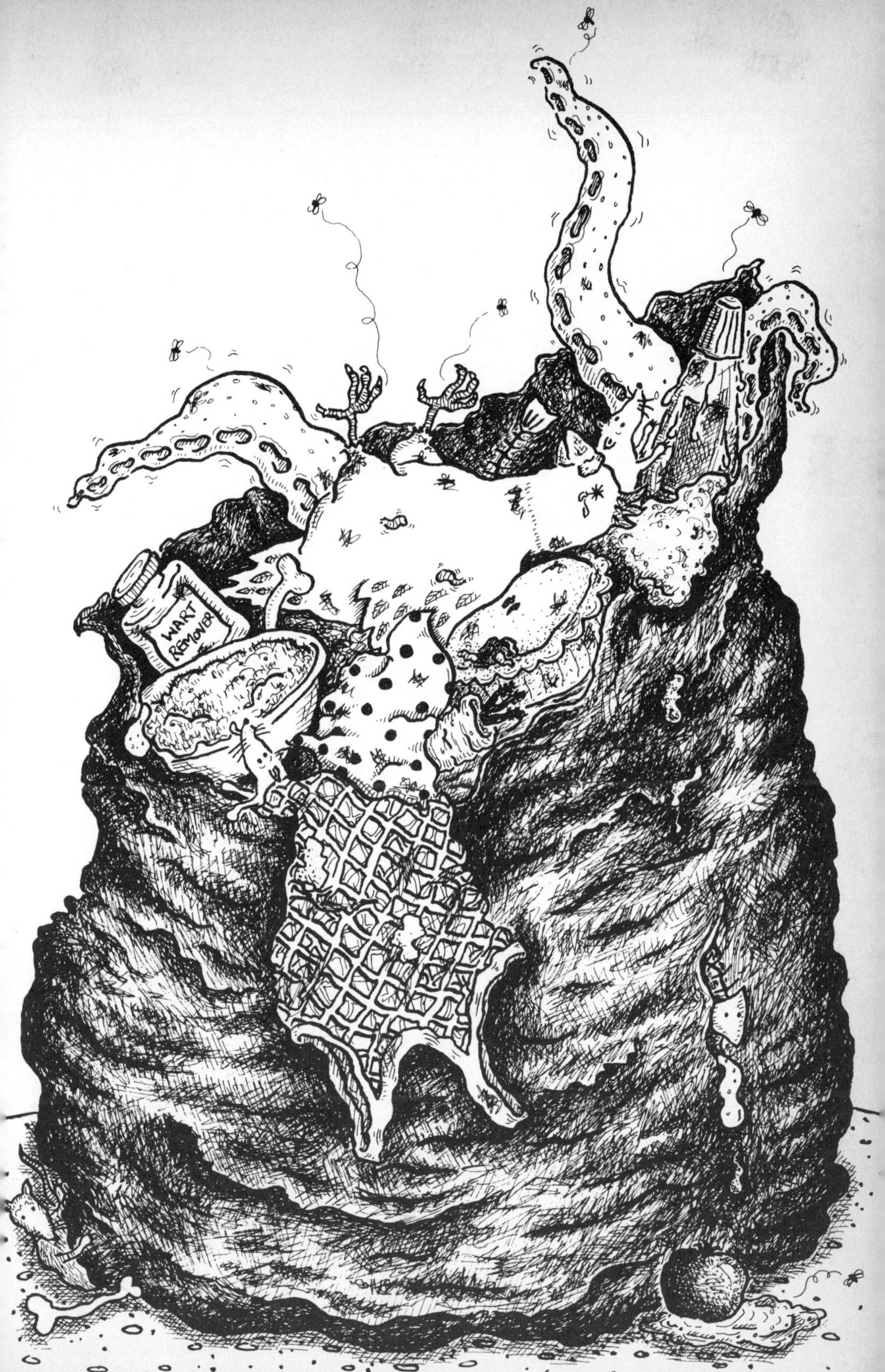
WART REMOVER

FATTY THE CAT

Fatty the cat
couldn't use his cat-flap
on account of his cat-flab

gargantuan hunk of feline gristle
bulbous-bellied, wobble-buttocked beast
Fatty would eat anything:
earwigs
carrier bags
y-fronts
rubber gloves
paving slabs
shrubbery
small dogs
mud
rocks
marigolds
and McDonald's takeaways

wouldn't touch his catfood, though

pumped to bursting
crammed with comestibles and kippers
Fatty pillaged the dinner from our plates
raided the pantry, larder, butcher's shop and
    fishmonger's
filched milk from the mouths of crying babes
and slunk away slobbering beneath a secret hedge
to finish off discarded fish and chip wrappings
insects, three willow warblers, an abandoned
    saveloy
and somebody's orange bobble-hat

this led to a sorry state of stoutness
a macroscopic moggy
a distended, dimpled dog-eater
dreaded by all living things (children, animals,

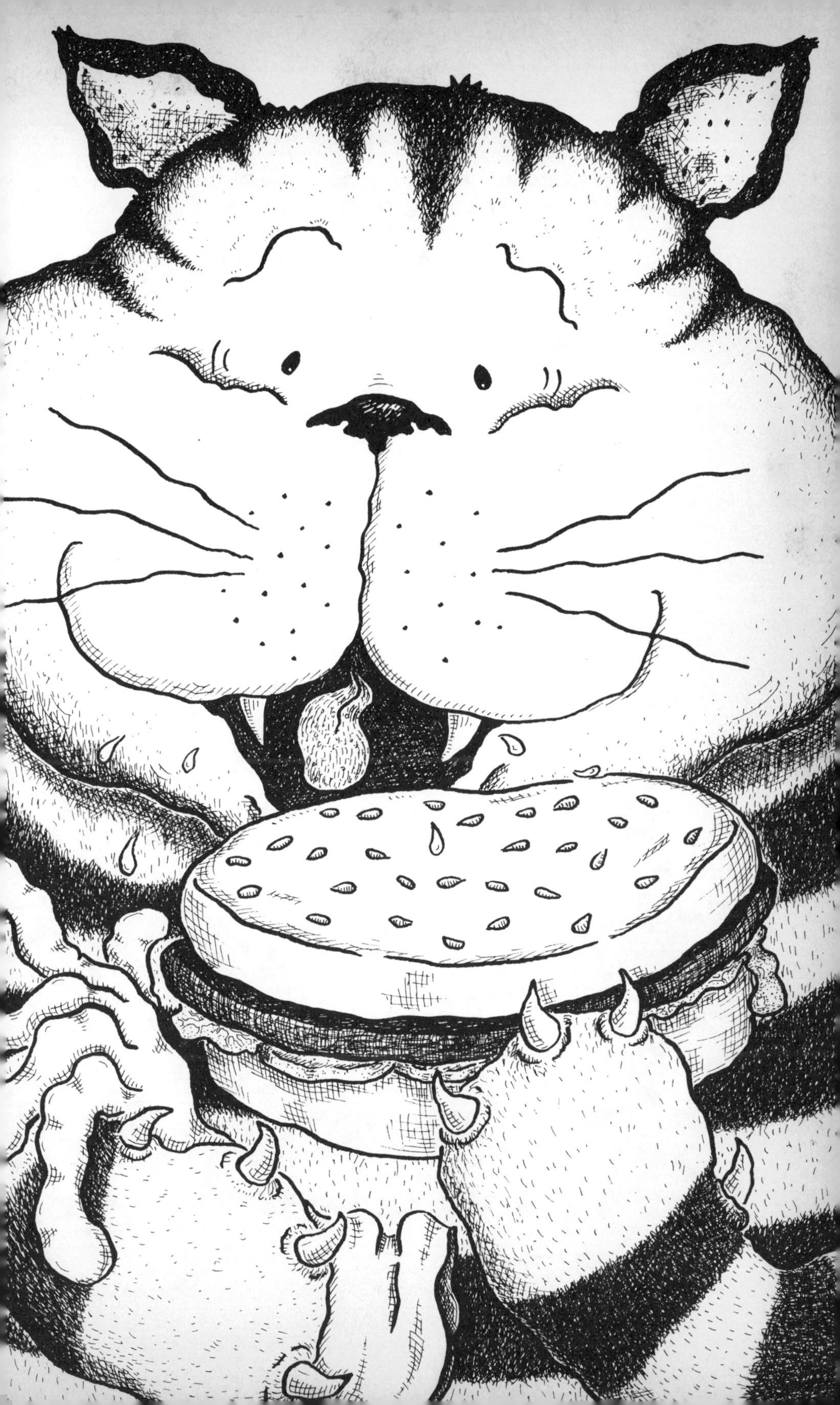

most adults)
Fatty suctioned edible portions of the universe
into the expanding contours of himself
then replete with macaroni cheese
apple turnovers and furtive frankfurters
Fatty assailed his cat-flap
failed
flabbygasted
well and truly stuck
like a polony
in a pencil sharpener

we had to call in the Fire Brigade
who pushed and pushed
and pulled and pulled
then shaking their heads
and shedding a tear
they popped Fatty with a pin

after the explosion
and the smoke
and confusion
we had a nice funeral
and thought of all the things he'd eaten:
spiders
bath towels
teabags
nettles
bricks
bric-a-brac
steak tartare
seagulls
marbles
caterpillars
cauliflower
cigarettes
polythene
and half a pound of caviar

Fatty would eat anything
edible, inedible
moving or non-moving
fast or slow
he was a feline dustbin
turned his nose up at nothing

wouldn't touch his catfood, though

LAUNDRY POEM

sploshity skuddy scum-scum whirr
billowy crumblies, plip plop ploop
bloomers a-clotted, latent smalls
soggy togs, crubbly socks
swishy tights elasticky
ballooned swirly whirlies
ickeroonies cheesecaked
snackered bio-bubbles
blubbery scrubbery frantic fizz
zip zip pillow wobble
KERUNDA
  ZONK
    STOP

VROOM SPIN

headachey squeedgy squiggle mangle
ouch oozings pressed double
errk-gawd-grind-gasp
white light
perfect wife
soft and lovely

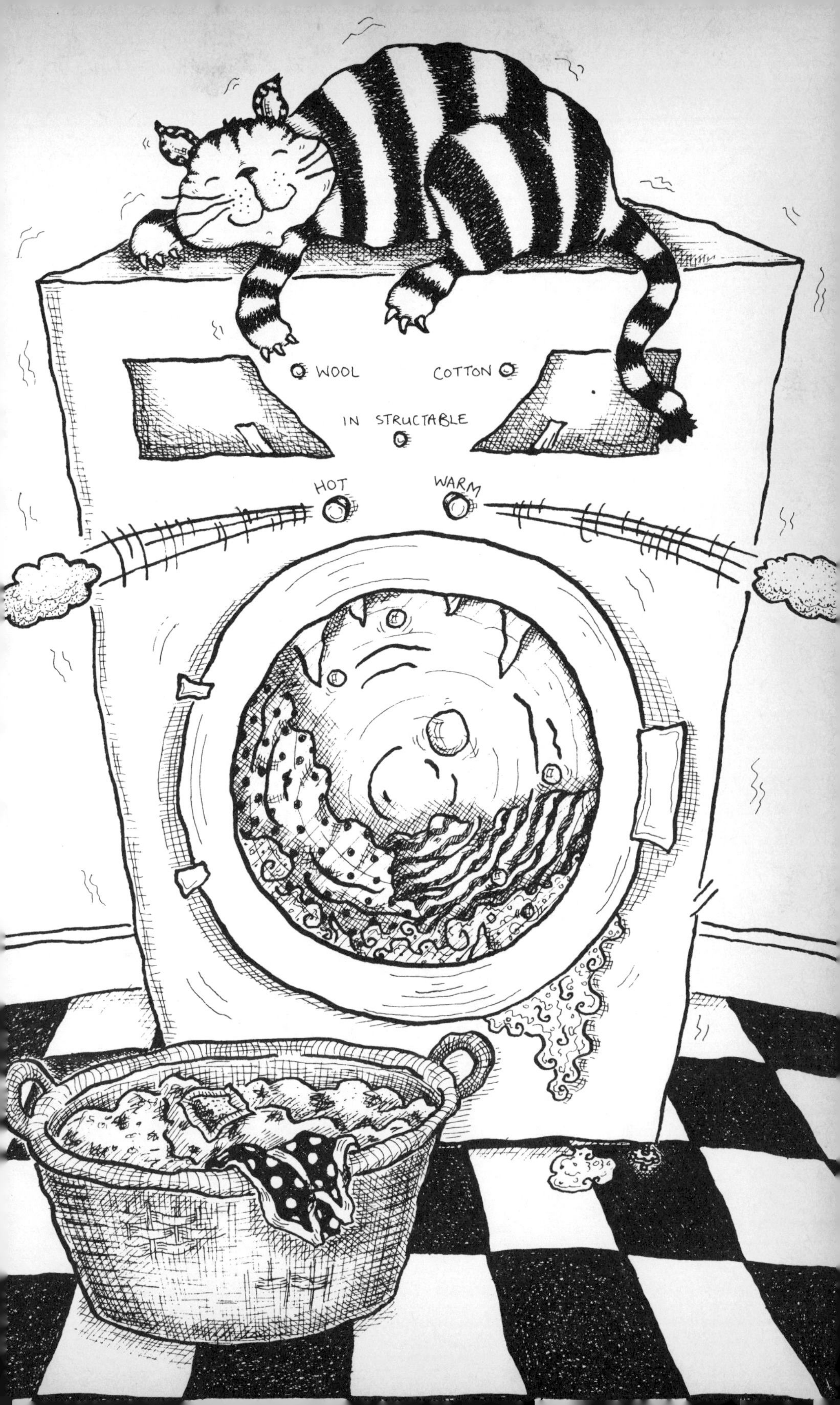
WOOL
COTTON
IN STRUCTABLE
HOT
WARM

FAST FOOD

sheep
pigs
ducks
dogs
zebras
ostriches
hot water bottles
bones
grit
gristle
rubber
sand
glass
rocks
trousers
cereal
fat
and cows
go in

sausages come out
  sausages come out
    sausages come out
      sausages come out

CELEBRATION

is daring
to be
who we are
it's like dancing
on table tops
while the world spins
and the fear stops
and the waves crash
and the stars glow
and the heart beats
and inside your head
you hear this song
rising
up
like laughter
rising
up
like a firework
soaring and weightless
to fill the whole sky
with joy

AT THE BOTTOM

Scrunge Shrimpkin
at the bottom of the ooze
lived on globularis
swollen with mud
pumped up with sloop
and sloppy despicables
   but I loved him

Scrunge Shrimpkin
pottled around on the river's slimy mattress
wallowed in ancient nasties
gorged his shovel-mouth with shrivelled death
and snored
like a motorbike throbbing over a cattle-grid
   but I loved him none-the-less

he lummered over the encrusted scum
like a scaly sea-adder, frothy-mouthed
full of gastric fumes and fish oil
fashioned in filth
sieving seaweed seed pods through his gut
knitting grey hummus out of algae-smothered crisp
   packets
wrinkled in the sog
Scrunge Shrimpkin pissed on his own foot
   but I loved him

   and it wasn't easy

'Hey Scrunge!' the kids used to shout
'He's got odd socks on!'
and Scrunge would slither back
in deep
down
faster than falling
and fasten his bulk onto the very bottom bog
cover his ugly ears with sog-clods
fiddle with his tubes

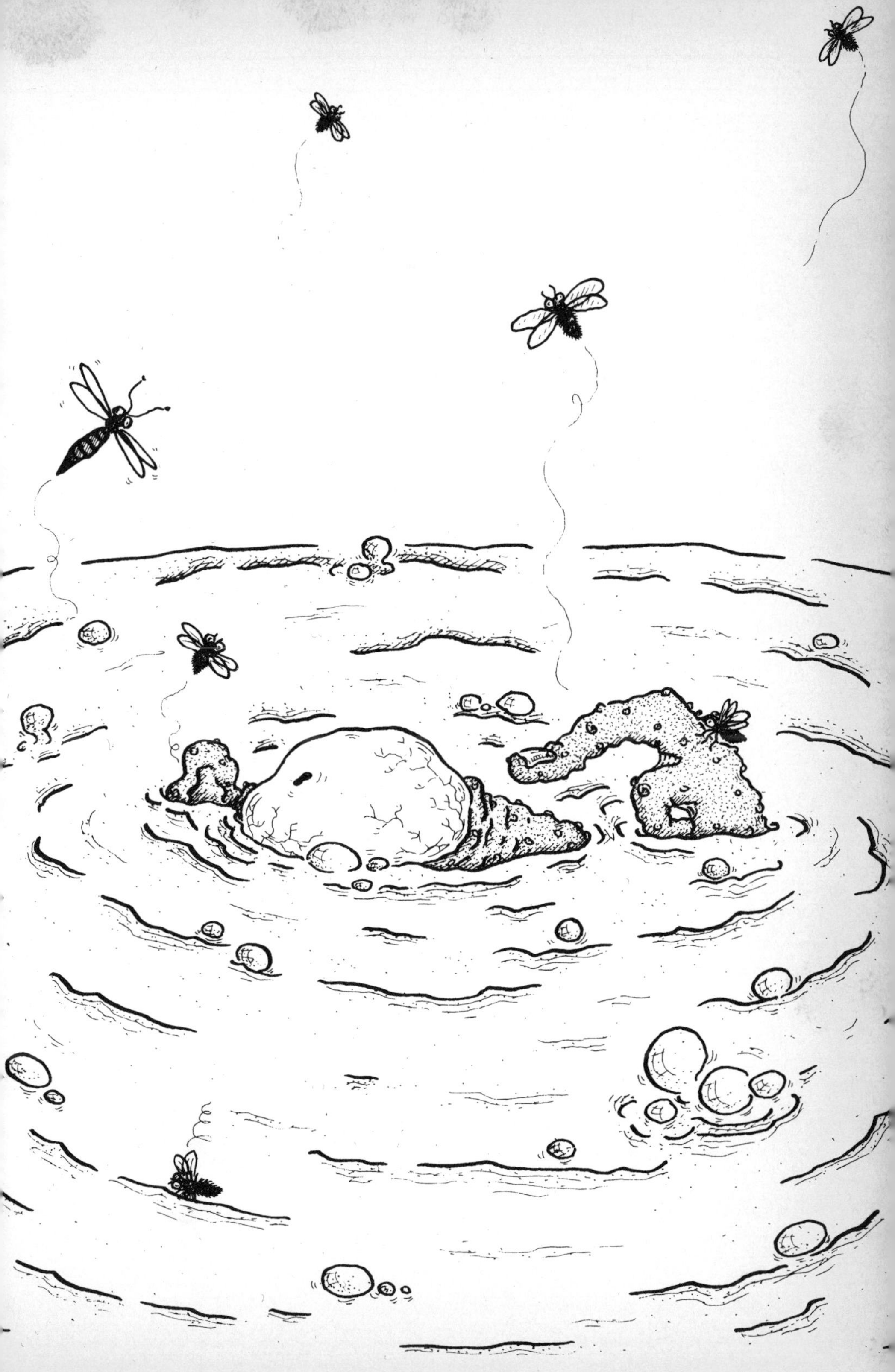

blow out little spores of sadness
and bellow into the black

vagabond abalones nibbled at his slack skin
the colour of lard
and demon dribblers raked his back
cooked in the bubbling squishy
Scrunge Shrimpkin
was al dente
but in the middle of a heave
he blew great gobbers of poison
at the skinny pilchards
and squirmed into the slush
safe
and
sound

Scrunge Shrimpkin
made a hole
in the glaucous, soft hills
combed his tendrils tickled with daphnia
snored
like a manatee with adenoids
and was buried at the bottom of the world

   but I loved him

TWO'S COMPANY

dog downstairs
goes woof woof woof woof
driving me crazy
with his woof woof woof

he sounds so miserable
he sounds so lonely
he seems to be telling me:
Life is Tough

dog downstairs
goes woof woof woof woof
whatever the weather
or the time of day
it's woof woof woof
in a syncopated rhythm
as he woof woof woofies
all his life away

I think I'll invite him
for a woof woof dinner
then together we can have a good
woof woof moan
yes together we will woof woof
woof woof woof woof

it's better than being
on your woof woof own

NOBODY

when nobody called
and nobody came
and nobody asked me how I felt
when nobody sent me Valentines
and nobody thought my heart could melt

when nobody rang
and nobody wrote
and nobody asked me out to play
I said to the butler
if nobody comes
tell him to go away

STATISTICS

my Uncle Jack thought he was safe
crossing roads

'You've more chance of getting cancer
than of getting run over,' he said

he died in 1978 at Whipsnade
run through by a rhinoceros
that didn't want its photograph taken
admittedly
there were no cars around at the time

KNIT-ONE PEARL-ONE

Aunty Bea comes to the dole office
To keep me company during the long hours
She is knitting a blanket out of bright red wool
It is twenty-five feet long and twelve-and-a-half feet wide
We have been there some time
The blanket covers everybody's knees:
The young and the old and the desperate
Keeping out the February chills
And the clicking of knitting needles
Works an hypnotic stillness
Numbing the pain of waiting

Aunty Bea's blanket gets longer and longer
And wider and wider
Until it is a soft red sea
Seething into the grimy stairway
Lapping at the interviewers' doors
Curling around the legs of bureaucrats
Undulating across those vast acres of hopelessness
Until finally
At the last row of knit-one pearl-one
It is cast off into a life of its own
To suffocate the Higher Executive Officers
With a swooping red Vengeance.

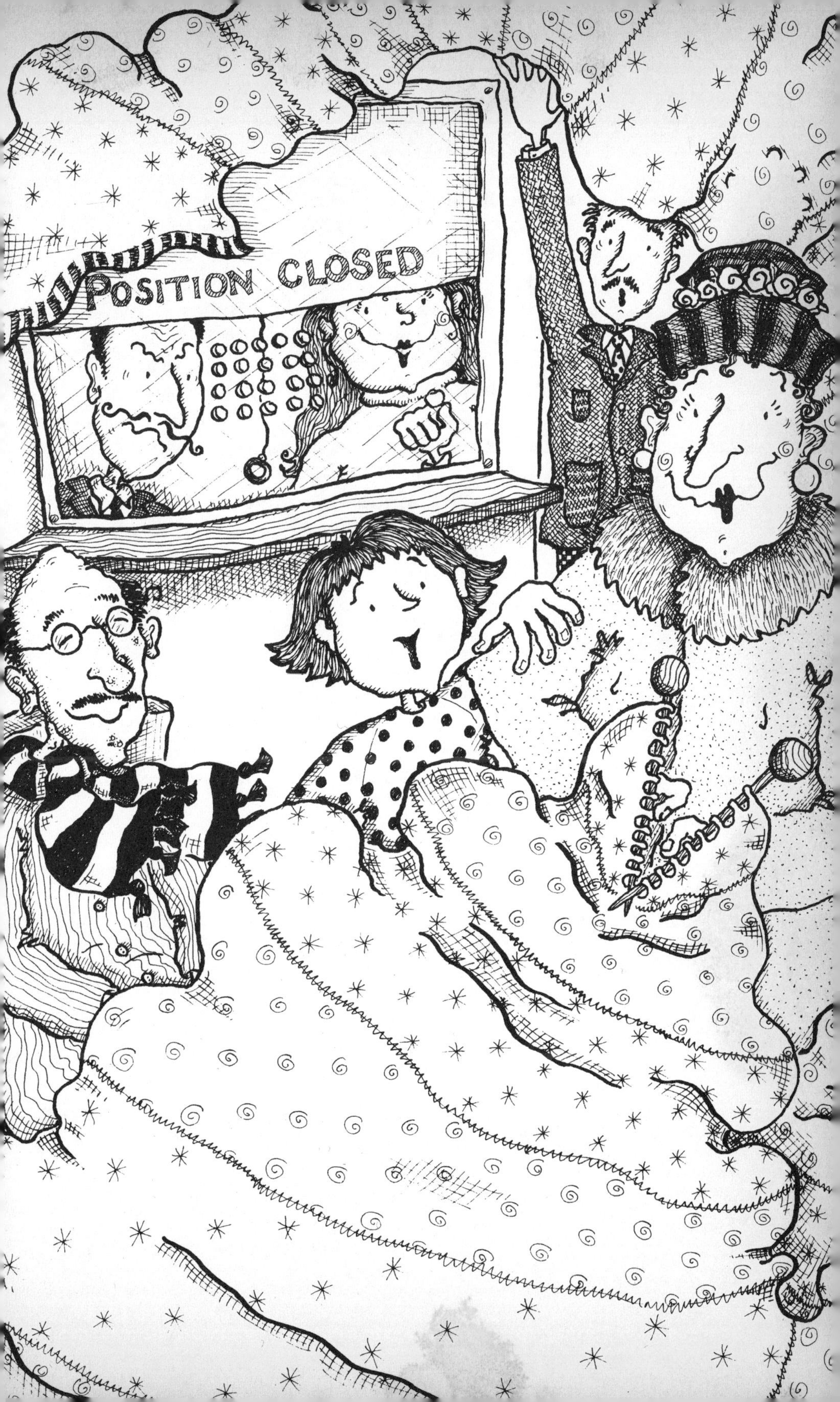
POSITION CLOSED

COMPUTER

If it can't cut hair and it can't darn socks
If it can't read books and it can't pick locks
If it can't tell jokes and it won't drink wine
If it can't hang washing on the washing line
If it can't bake bread and it can't make stew
If it can't go to Safeways and stand in a queue
If it can't drive a car and it can't ride a horse
If it can't make spaghetti with bolognese sauce
If it can't have fun and it can't quite smile
If it won't let its hair down once in a while
If it can't give me cuddles when I feel uptight
What use is a computer on a cold dark night?

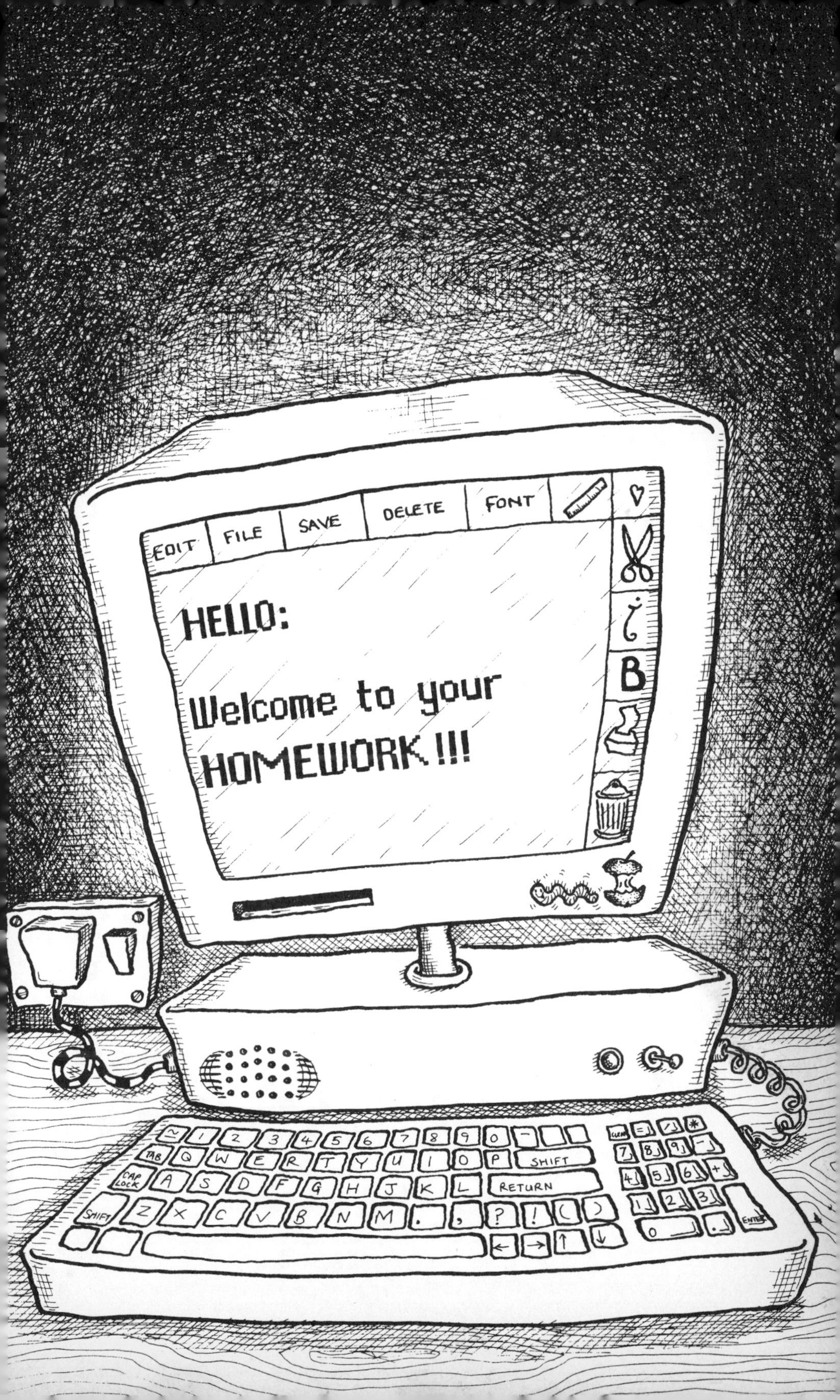
EDIT
FILE
SAVE
DELETE
FONT
B
HELLO:
Welcome to your
HOMEWORK!!!

JIGSAW

when you have done the Swiss Alps
and the skiers
and the fir trees
and the mountain cafe
and the blue lake
and the children
and the floating birds
and the drifting clouds
and the birdsong
and the atmosphere
and the silent echo
and everything fits together perfectly

I want to put in the last piece of sky

LAST DAY IN BROADSTAIRS

on the beach
we dug holes
frantically
hoping to reach China

'Please, Mum, don't send us back to Woolwich'

inevitable return
to grim streets and sunken hearts
to a skinhead sun glowering
in a mouldering sky of stiff-fisted cloud
to gaps where forget-me-nots and skylarks
never came
and there was no sea
to gently whisper our names

at night
I tried to remember the sound of gulls
and thought my heartbeat
was the rhythm of the ocean

A LOSS

You cannot see the wood
For the trees
And the wood has all been burned
And the trees have lost their leaves
And the roots are old and useless
And the branches broken
And the birds won't nest there
And there isn't a sound
And even the badgers think the ground too hard
And even the toads think the moss too damp
And even the starlings think the worms too ill

At a loss
We planted acorns on another hill

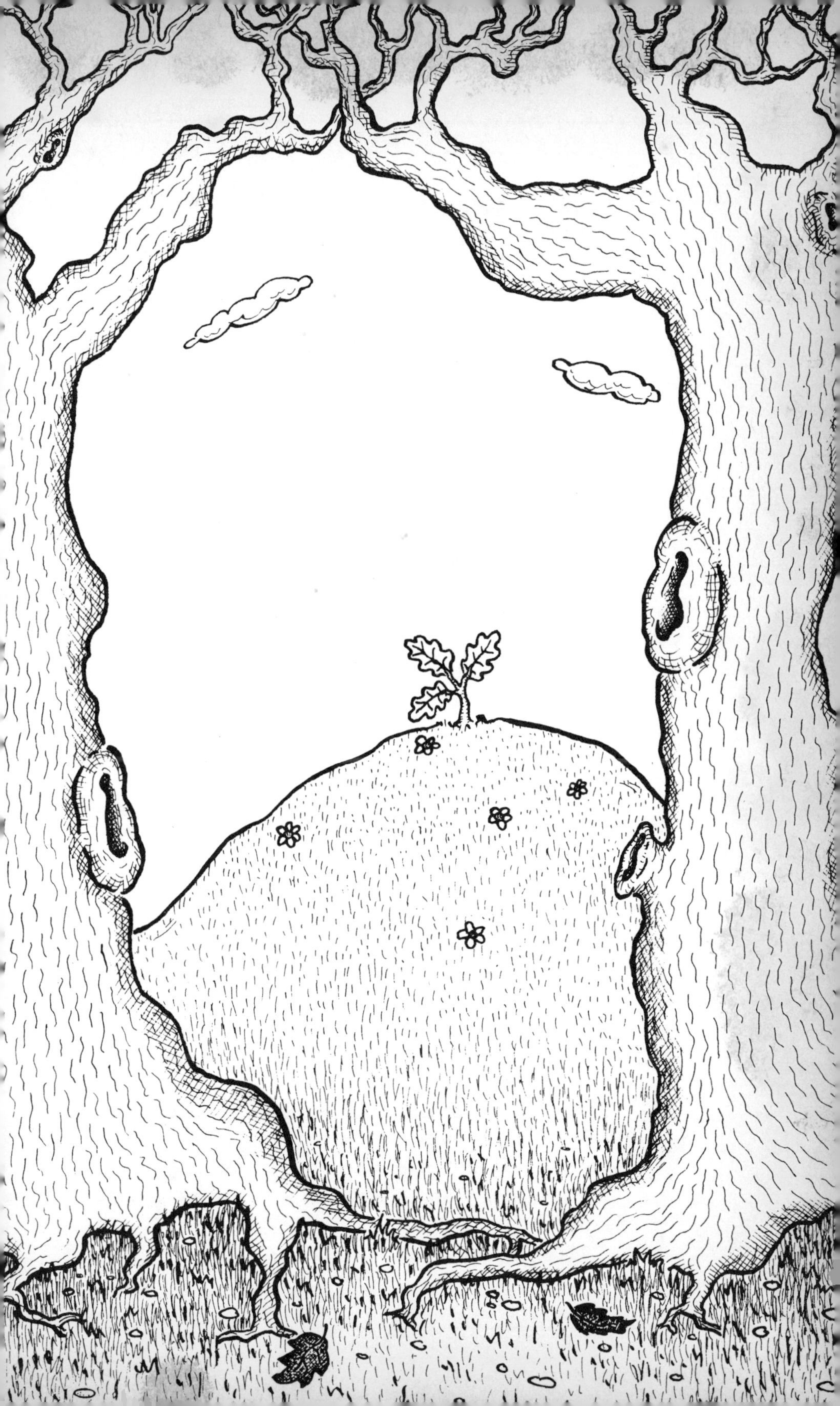

NATIONAL POETRY DAY

Will there be juggling and jiving and jelly?
Or boring renditions of Wordsworth and Shelley?
Will there be jamming and big jamborees?
Will poets do cartwheels and hang from the trees?
Will there be parties and picnics and prizes?
Will there be chocolate fudge and choc ices?
Will there be rhythm and rapping and rhyme?
Will people be having a wonderful time?
   On Poetry Day. On Poetry Day
   People shout Yee Haw
   And Hip Hip Hooray!
   Let the Power of Poetry show us the way
   On Poetry Day. On Poetry Day.

Will housewives stop cleaning and have time to dream?
Will bankers shut shop and begin the Beguine?
Will stockbrokers stock up on beautiful verses?
Will hospital patients get poems from nurses?
Will couples spout couplets and stop having rows?
Will farmers recite Kubla Khan to their cows?
Will cafes give poems with each cup of tea?
Will bricklayers start reading Ann Ziety?
   On Poetry Day. On Poetry Day
   People shout Yee Haw
   And Hip Hip Hooray!
   Let the Power of Poetry show us the way
   On Poetry Day. On Poetry Day.

Will plumbers stop plumbing and plunge into verse?
Will people with bad tempers rhythmically curse?
Will convicts give poetry in their defence?
Will sausages sizzle with soft sibilance?
Will doggies spout doggerel and stop chasing cats?

NATIONAL POETRY DAY

Will haddocks mouth ballads and wear green
   cravats?
Will judges on hearing the fresh evidence
Issue the world with a poetic licence?
   On Poetry Day. On Poetry Day
   People shout Yee Haw
   And Hip Hip Hooray!
   Let the Power of Poetry show us the way
   On Poetry Day. On Poetry Day.

Will babies start gurgling and cooing in rhyme?
Will burglars stop burgling and start doing time?
Will piggies stop squealing and finding the muse,
get out of their pig-pens to pen some haikus?
Will nasty dictators dictate villanelles?
Will soldiers throw parties instead of bombshells?
Will Presidents, Kings and Prime Ministers all
Give up their positions to answer the call?
   On Poetry Day. On Poetry Day
   People shout Yee Haw
   And Hip Hip Hooray!
   Let the Power of Poetry show us the way
   On Poetry Day. On Poetry Day.

   Yee Haw!